OUTSELL

THE GUARANTEED COMPETITIVE ADVANTAGE FOR YOUR SALES TEAM

INTRODUCING THE SALES P.A.R. EXCELLENCE STRATEGY

By Bill Burnett

Outsell: The Guaranteed Competitive
Advantage for your Sales Team

Copyright © 2018 Bill Burnett
All rights reserved.
ISBN: : 1986232743
ISBN-13:978-1986232746

DEDICATION

I dedicate this book to my lovely wife Linda who has been supportive of my endeavors through thick and thin.

Table of Contents

Table of Contents i

Introduction 1

It Pays To Ask 9

A Strange Mind 17

A Question Is Worth A Thousand Statements. ... 49

The Peak/End Rule 55

Question Of Intent 71

The Counterfactual Hypothetical 81

Mixing a Message 117

A Sales Force Marches On Its Questions. 131

ACKNOWLEDGMENTS

I would like to thank the many friends who used *The Peak Interview* techniques to get their next jobs, and then brought them into their new companies as part of their sales strategy. A number of these experienced sales executives have encouraged me to put this book together.

I would like to thank my son Charles who contributed by editing early drafts with his gifted editing hand. Some marvelous and generous people I know have helped make the book better by reading drafts and making suggestions as well as finding many typographical errors. They are: Ty Foren, whose turn-around time for editing was phenomenal, Todd Perlman, Paul Bowles, Ken Shearer, Lauren Kelliher, and Greg Stellflue for their expertise at catching errors and making suggestions. I have a special thanks to Lauren Kelliher who kept the theme of the whole work in mind while employing her obvious love of grammar and attention to detail to create masterful edits. If you need a top-notch professional editor, send me a note and I will put you in touch with Lauren. Thanks to all of you. Of course, for any errors that remain, I take all the credit. If you find an error, let me know and I'll include your name here in the next update. bill@manuparx.com

Finally, I'd like to thank Daniel Kahneman whose work has allowed me to ask a question like:

How does deliberately increasing the amount of pain a patient feels in a colonoscopy lead to more effective sales to prospective clients?

Introduction

Seven years ago I wrote *The Peak Interview.* It is the predecessor book to this book. As soon as it was out, it created something unexpected.

It was originally written to show off my company's process for finding new competitive advantage for our clients. As a product, it was difficult to sell. Prospects wanted to hear success stories, and most of our success stories were esoteric to an industry or company. I wanted a good case study that everyone could more easily appreciate. Ideally it would be one where many people had already exhausted every opportunity for finding competitive advantage.

From a list of possible choices, I selected the problem, '*How do you create competitive advantage in the job interview?*' It was a good choice because all of my prospects understand the job interview. They know that everyone tries to establish competitive advantage over their unknown rivals. Moreover, there are thousands of professionals helping these job seekers to create and communicate their competitive advantage. Hence, you wouldn't expect any single stone to be left unturned.

Yet, the process my company uses to find competitive advantage turned over a couple of hidden and useful stones. I then wrote-up the case study and, because it leverages the Peak/End Rule, called it *The Peak Interview.* My intention was to use it as a business card handout. A book gives consultants more credibility. The book, of course, reveals the answer to the question, '*How do you create competitive advantage in the job interview?*'

Quite by accident it became something other than a business card handout. A friend and business owner read the book. It turned out that he also ran a church's employment ministry to help people in their job searches (we were just coming out of the Great Recession). One day, a guest speaker cancelled at the last minute, and he asked me if I could put together a handful of slides covering my book and present to the group, which I did. A week later the phone rang. It was a community job-search networking group and I did another presentation for them. The phone has yet to stop ringing. Since that first talk, I've delivered it about 175 times. I've had a lot of fun giving this free presentation to thousands of job seekers.

It has its rewards. I get emails from people who've used *The Peak Interview* process and they generously attribute their success to the techniques in the book, including my three adult children, which is deeply gratifying to me as a father!

Among the people who've used the techniques to land a job are quite a few <u>sales people</u>. Many from that group, not only used the techniques to land a job, but then incorporated the techniques into their sales strategy. Their insight revealed the job interview is actually nothing more than a sales call.

It's not just sales people who use the techniques to win business. Len Green, who is CEO of Haygarth Consulting LLC, tells this story:

"We knew we were in fourth place among four companies competing for a prospect's business.

On the flight out to visit the prospect I reread the book and based on the techniques in the book, formulated a couple of questions to ask the prospect.

I used the questions, and all I can say is that just before we boarded our flight home, the client texted us the good news they'd chosen us!"

OUTSELL

Over the past five years many of these people who've used the techniques to sell, have encouraged me to write a book that ports the techniques from The Peak Interview into a regular face-to-face sales call. Their encouragement led to this book.

Two of the question types discussed later in this short book are the Counterfactual Hypothetical Question, and The Peak/End Question. Both job candidates and sales people have used these two question types for the past seven years. Thousands of times these two question types have proven themselves as effective in driving favorable decisions, from hiring managers to prospects. The third question type, the intent question, emerged as a useful technique since *The Peak Interview* was published. Its effectiveness is based on the experiments done by behavioral economists and psychologists.

I'm calling the tools within this book 'The Sales P.A.R.[1] Excellence Strategy'. (Based upon, and complementary to an a business operating methodology called 'Manufacturing P.A.R. Excellence.' Like this book it is also based upon proven practices which leverage the sciences of: behavioral economics, psychology, and neuroscience.)

The techniques in this book are not intended to replace your existing sales strategies. Rather, I encourage you to figure out how you might use one or more of the techniques to enhance your ability to ask influential questions, build relationships, and close deals.

Cognitive impact is about addressing the necessary elements of decision-making. Decision-making involves both rational and emotional processes, as well as conscious

---

[1] "Par excellence" is a term that signifies "above all; preeminently, to a degree of excellence; beyond comparison." As an acronym P.A.R. stands for Propositions, Answers, Relationships. Influential questions use Propositions, Answers are more influential than questions, and Relationships are always the good salesperson's goal.

and subconscious activities. A sales call is always about cognitive impact. There is a difference between cognitive impact and manipulating. Producing cognitive impact is the capacity to affect the actions, behavior, and opinions of others. Manipulation involves managing outcomes through unfair or false tactics. Essentially, if someone's intentions are bad, they are probably trying to manipulate. In this book, I am assuming your intentions are good and your interest is in how to create a bit more cognitive impact by being more effective in how you communicate the truth to prospects. You are not motivated to manipulate.

Could these techniques be used for bad ends? Yes. In fact when I talk about the Counterfactual Hypothetical later in this book, I will show you a case where it's been used dishonestly to create unfair advantage in a presidential primary.

It Pays To Ask

Over the years, I've noticed three primary approaches sales people used with me when I've been the recipient of a sales call:

- Launching into a formal sales presentation
- Talking about their company and their products (a lot)
- Asking questions and telling stories

Certainly, there are times when a formal sales presentation is called for. Personally, I've never liked being on the receiving end. And I know salespeople who won't use a formal presentation. They feel a sale is entirely about the relationship with the customer, and a formal presentation can work against them. I'm not going to talk about formal presentations here.

If your approach is to talk about your company and your products, this probably is not the book for you. I do recommend a handful of books that would be helpful to someone currently using this sales approach. They include five books that I encourage any salesperson to read: *Socratic Selling* by Kevin Daley, *Start With No* by Jim Camp, *Pulling In The Same Direction* by Barry Fowell and Chris Behan, which talks about aligning sales and marketing, *Made to Stick* by Chip and Dan Heath, and *Put The Win Back In Your Sales* by Dan Kreutzer.

If you're doing all the talking, you're on the wrong side of the table.

The best salespeople ask questions. When I ask why they use questions in a sale, they respond with three primary reasons:
- To qualify the prospect
- To find the prospect's pain points
- To get to know the prospect

Most sales people choose one of these three

as their primary focus, but pursue all three purposes. All three share the objective of information gathering. Some salespeople behave as though the prospect were an adversary. They duck and weave through the prospect's business situation in the hope of eventually backing them into a buying position.

However, the most adept salespeople I know always ask questions to get to know the prospect, find some common ground, and start to create a relationship, in addition to understanding the prospect's needs.

Information gathering is important in a sales call. Sales people use this information later in the sales call to influence the decision the prospect will make. Cognitive impact is the objective. Recent science tells us that questions themselves, can be powerful as tools of cognitive impact. In this book I will show how questions, and their answers, can influence the prospect's decision-making.

I came, I asked, I closed.

The Sales P.A.R. Excellence Strategy employs three kinds of influencing questions. These questions are used first to manage cognitive impact and second to gather information. If you had to choose between cognitive impact and information gathering, you should choose cognitive impact. Studies in behavioral economics and psychology (which I site later in the book) have shown us that three specific types of questions can be extraordinarily influential[2], particularly at cognitive impact levels:

- The Peak/End Question
- The Intent Question
- The Counterfactual Hypothetical Question

I will describe how to use each of these later in this book, along with the science behind how we know these types of

---

[2] The influence is so strong a team of investigators felt, *"that it should be forbidden to ask questions for the sake of creating an advantage."* Pandelaere, Mario & Dewitte, Siegfried. (2005). Is this a Question? Not for Long. The Statement Bias. Katholieke Universiteit Leuven, Open Access publications from Katholieke Universiteit Leuven. P.21

questions can be powerful influencers.

Further, we can use questions to accomplish three other important things:

- Properly formed questions can cause the prospect to lower his or her cognitive guard.
- Questions can trigger the emotional center of the prospect's brain. Neuroscience suggests the emotional centers of the brain are also where making choices and forming decisions takes place.
- Questions get the prospect to reveal whether our cognitive impact is gaining traction.

Stories

There are many books on the use of stories in sales. The fundamental theme in these books is when you tell well-crafted stories; they are a powerful way to get your message across. **This is true.**

Some of these *how to sell* books focus on the stories you tell to influence the buying decision. It is one thing to use stories to get your message to be understood, but it is something different to make your message influential. These books suggest that, "Your stories do the selling for you". The underlying guiding theme that drives the content of these books, is the idea that, "Being heard is by far the most important ingredient for influence." **This is not true.**

Your story is certainly essential to delivering information. In this book I use my company's stories to help my prospects build the narratives of their stories. I will show it's not the story you tell that does the selling: I**t is the story your prospect tells. The story your prospect tells is your most influential selling tool.**

We will tell stories to give our prospects the narrative elements needed for them to construct the story we want to hear them tell. I will cover how to craft a story, how you set it up, how you tell it, and how you end it. From now on, you will use stories to give your prospects the narrative content for the story you want them to tell.

Science is the core of the Sales P.A.R. Excellence Strategy. To develop the strategy, I've combined insights from behavioral economics, psychology and a bit of neuroscience. It turns out the human brain has a strange decision engine. Nevertheless, it is the decision engine that we have to deal with. Its strangeness is next.

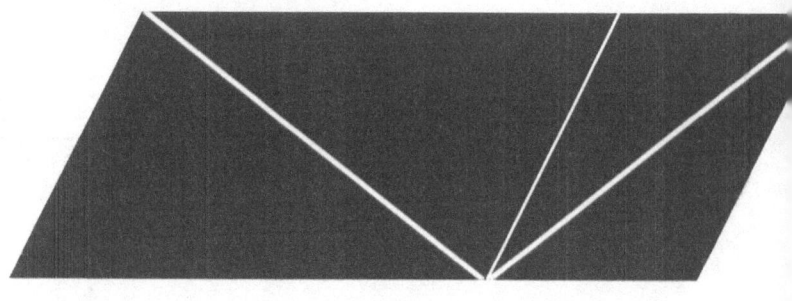

Strange Mind

Note to the reader: If your interest is solely how to make you sales questions more influential, and you're not curious about the science behind why this works, you should skip this chapter.

When dealing with the human brain's decision-making apparatus there's good news and bad news.

The bad news is the apparatus is peculiar. The good news is it's predictably peculiar. We can use the predictable nature of the brain's decision-making apparatus to our advantage.

Most of us have confidence in our perceptions, in our thinking, and in our decision-making. But is this confidence warranted? Over the past forty years, behavioral economists and psychologists have been showing us many ways in which our confidence is probably unjustified.

Both the way humans perceive the world and how we form opinions, beliefs, and decisions showcase interesting quirks. A classic visual example is the Sander's Parallelogram (at the beginning of this chapter). Most people see the diagonal white line through the parallelogram on the left as longer than the diagonal on the right. If you measure them, the two are identical.

Perhaps a more convincing example is from Roger Shepard, as shown in the image below[3]. Almost everyone sees the dark

---

[3] Shepard, Roger Newland. Mind Sights: Original Visual Illusions, Ambiguities, and Other Anomalies, with a Commentary on the Play of Mind in Perception and Art. New York: Freeman, 1990.

OUTSELL

parallelogram (tabletop marked 'X') on the left as being twice as long as it is wide, while seeing the other dark parallelogram (tabletop marked 'Y') as more square. In the chart under the images, choose the answer that best matches what you see.

Table	X	Y
Answer	Length/Width	Length/Width
A	3/1	1/1
B	2/1	2/1
C	3/1	2/1

Most people would look at you like you're crazy if you said the parallelograms are the same size. If you want to check, then photocopy the page, cut out one of the dark parallelograms and place it over the other.

Surprise! They're the same size, exactly.

Our brains are designed to interpret information, like visual imagery, in a way that is useful in navigating the world. This illusion is a simple example of a situation where the decision-making apparatus in our brains can lead us to an incorrect conclusion.

Substitution

Psychologists have noticed that people are rarely without opinions even around complex issues. Regardless of expertise, or how much they've thought about the issues, most people have a position on governmental and economic policy, the contents of the news, and on the value of a particular scientific finding. We are rarely stumped in the face of complexity; we often substitute one thing for another in coming up with an answer to complex questions.

An example is the question: "How happy are you generally?" Psychological investigators in Germany asked students a set of questions including these two:

OUTSELL

"How happy are you with your life in general?"

"How many dates did you have last month?"[4]

It turned out when they ask these two questions in this order, there was no correlation between how happy the students were and the number of dates they had been on in the last month. However, when they asked the two questions in reverse order, there was a high correlation between the number of dates students had had and how happy they said they were. This is an example of 'attribute substitution'[5]. Students let their feelings around how many dates they've been on act as substitute for how happy they should feel.

---

[4] Strack, Fritz, Leonard L. Martin, and Norbert Schwarz. "Priming and Communication: Social Determinants of Information Use in Judgments of Life Satisfaction." *European Journal of Social Psychology*. 1988

[5] Kahneman, Daniel, and Shane Frederick. "Representativeness Revisited: Attribute Substitution in Intuitive Judgment." *Heuristics and Biases* (n.d.): 49-81.

Taking Shortcuts

When I work with leadership teams I use the problem below to illustrate this substitution phenomenon.

Miles per Gallon of Gas	MPG at 75 MPH*	MPG at 55 MPH
Car 1	30.7	39.9
Car 2	36.5	51.9
Car 3	17.8	23.8
Car 4	25.9	34.6
*MPH = Miles Per Hour; MPG = Miles Per Gallon		

The question is: if the four drivers of the four cars slow down from their normal highway speed of 75MPH to a more moderate 55MPH for the next 10,000 miles, which driver will save the most money on gasoline for their car?

About eighty percent of respondents will eyeball this, and guess based on the apparent difference in miles per gallon (MPG). Others will actually calculate the difference in MPG, coming up with:

OUTSELL

Car Driven	Difference in MPG between 55 and 75 MPH
Car 1	9.2
Car 2	15.4
Car 3	6
Car 4	8.7

Now they have a more precise calculation showing car 2 has the biggest improvement in miles per gallon. This is just putting more effort into an intuitive, but incorrect, approach. Actually, putting this extra effort into solving the problem can make you more confident in your conclusion. However, both groups are substituting the MPG for the cost, thinking that since Car 2 has the biggest improvement in miles per gallon by slowing down to 55MPH, it will produce the most savings.

The problem isn't about an improvement in miles per gallon. It's about saving money on gas when you drive 10,000 miles at a slower speed. Even when I point this out to teams, most team members will elect not to put the extra effort into solving the problem correctly. It takes work, and chances are that you, the reader, won't do it either. Now that I've hinted the correct answer is not Car 2, you're more likely to take a guess (perhaps going in the opposite direction and choosing Car 3) than figuring out how to solve the problem.

The cautionary tale here is that this natural inclination to conserve mental energy (often called 'mental laziness' by psychologists) is almost always present in team problem solving. People tend to use intuition and heuristics (e.g. rules of thumb, estimates, metaphors, substitutions etc.) rather than deep thinking. The loudest voice in the room frequently has the laziest brain. The solutions often are okay. If you want solutions that are better than 'okay', you need a disciplined process[6]. Therefore, during a sales call you want to be careful not to make an argument that requires

---

[6] Interestingly, in implementing the P.A.R. Excellence operating methodology, I find this is a bigger issue for manufacturing teams than other teams. People in manufacturing tend to solve problems continuously all day long, and get into the habit of using quick-and-dirty solutions. This is a hard habit to break.

deep thinking on the part of the prospect. The prospect will not do it.

Now, you might be thinking to yourself, that lazy brain problem is probably true for other teams, but it's not true for our team, *"We're really good at problem-solving."* You're probably kidding yourself.

Back in the year I graduated high school, the now famous duo of Tversky and Kahneman ran an experiment using 84 trained statistical experts at a meeting of the Mathematical Psychology Society and the American Psychological Association.[7]

The 84 experts were asked about their level of confidence for the accuracy test results of a small sample size, later confirmed with a second test comprised of a sample size half as big as the first when the represented population was large. A substantial majority of these statisticians reported a significantly high level of confidence in the

---

[7] Tversky, A. & Kahneman, D. 1971. Belief in the law of small numbers. *Psychological Bulletin*. 76. 105-110.

reliability of the findings; after all, they had two test groups showing similar results.

A simple probability calculation that each of these math wizards could have done in a few seconds on a napkin would have shown a different, and much lower level of confidence. They should have known this. They chose to ignore the disciplines of their field, went with their 'gut', and felt confident with their incorrect answers.[8]

Tversky and Kahneman discovered that even highly trained experts tend to rely on a spontaneous, intuitive, and effortless, approach to answering questions. It is a tendency of the 'lazy brain' to bypass an approach that is deliberate, rule-governed,

---

[8] If you've read Malcolm Gladwell's *Blink* where he discusses "go with your gut" decisions from psychologist Gary Klein (the story of the fireman who sensed danger). It has been a debate between Klein who bases his conclusions on anecdotal evidence, and Kahneman who prefers to figure out how to design an experiment. Both worked to reconcile their positions: https://www.digitaltonto.com/2012/when-should-we-go-with-our-gut-and-when-should-we-look-before-we-leap/

and effortful (which these statisticians knew was the only reliable approach). If highly trained statisticians use intuitive short cuts with confidence, you can anticipate your team's confidence in their answers is likely to be equally unreliable.

Kahneman points out, "The best we can do is a compromise: learn to recognize situations in which mistakes are likely, and try harder to avoid significant mistakes when the stakes are high...and that it is easier to recognize other people's mistakes than our own."[9]

In our sales strategy, we are trying to address this 'mental laziness' by making it easy for our prospect to reach the right conclusion.

System One and System Two

Behavioral Economists study how we make

---

[9] Kahneman, Daniel. *Thinking, Fast and Slow*. New York: Farrar, Straus and Giroux, 2015, p.45

economic and other decisions[10]. Following the work mentioned above, Kahneman developed a model of decision-making. It suggests that two systems are involved whenever we think about anything. System One is the automatic part of the brain where answers emerge without us putting forth any effort. System Two is where effortful thinking takes place.

An example of the difference between System One and System Two is something called *Compound Remote Associate Problems*, or C.R.A.P. Mark Jung-Beeman at Northwestern University, and Edward Bowden, now at the University of Wisconsin, Parkside, compiled these problems. They created a list of puzzles based on how quickly people get them. Some puzzles people solve quickly and effortlessly (System One). For example, what word is associated with each of these

---

[10] Strictly speaking, behavioral economist would be focused on economic decisions. But the field was started by psychologist who are interested in decision-making more broadly, e.g. happiness, meaning, identity, love...

three words: *man/stop/wrist*? The answer is '*watch*', as in watchman, stopwatch, and wristwatch.

Try these four, each with a different common word:

cottage/swiss/cake
rocking/wheel/high
cream/skate/water
show/life/row

Chances are, with at least one of these, you experienced a brain snap, where the answer (*cheese, chair, ice, boat*) just popped into your head. It's as if your brain does something you don't control or truly understand. It is as if something deeper in your brain broadcasts the right answer to your consciousness. But stop for a moment and consider the broadside of processing the brain must do to make a broadjump to the right answer!

Now with the following puzzles you may feel more in control of the process. Most of us don't get these quickly or easily, if at all.

If you get even one, you're doing better than I did.

cast/side/jump
reading /service/stick
shadow/chart/drop
land/hand/house

Here you may have found yourself doing a great deal more searching through your mental dictionary of all the words associated with each of the words in the four puzzles. It is slow and effortful. It is System Two at work. If you got the first one, *broadcast/broadside/broadjump*, it's because of a different bit of psychology, called priming[11]. Email me and tell me if you got the cast/side/jump question and I'll give you the answers to the other three: bill@manuparx.com

Humans naturally conserve personal

---

[11] In a paragraph above I inserted the words broadcast, broadside and broadjump in an odd way that may have caused your brain to pay a moment's attention to them. That made them more accessible when you got to the C.R.A.P puzzle. Don't worry though, most people still don't come up with the answer.

energy. The brain is said to consume 20 percent of the body's energy every day[12]. We are naturally inclined to conserve our thinking energy and let System One come up with an answer to a problem whenever it can.

For example, take this problem:
Together, a basketball backboard and ball cost $110.
The backboard costs $100 more than the ball.
How much does the ball cost?

If you are like 99 percent of the population the first number that pops into your brain is $10. That's System One finding the easy answer for you. This is an intuitive answer.[13] When that happens it makes this

---

[12] The calculation is based on half-a-century-old Hodgkin–Huxley equations that used a squid's brain. More recent research suggests the human brain may be three times more efficient than a squid's brain, and thus the energy consumption may be less. See: Alle, H., A. Roth, and J. R. P. Geiger. "Energy-Efficient Action Potentials in Hippocampal Mossy Fibers." *Science* 325.5946 (2009): 1405-408.

[13] Kahneman, Daniel. *Thinking, Fast and Slow*. New York: Farrar, Straus and Giroux, 2015, p.45

simple math problem more difficult to solve. ($10 is incorrect, by the way.) A similar problem was given to university students at three Ivy League schools. More than 50 percent of these students got it wrong, while at less selective schools more than 80 percent of student settled on the intuitive, but incorrect, answer.

This little problem is a great example of how our brain can fool us. It jumps to the easy conclusion most of the time. The basketball backboard and ball problem shows us an example of Daniel Kahneman's concept of System One and System Two thinking.[14] System One is our eager-beaver problem solver.

Letting System One make decisions is fine for most decisions because most decisions are of little consequence. But System One is fast because it employs rules of thumb. It takes a problem and sees if it can match it up to a previously solved problem where the pattern looks the same. If System One

---

[14] Ibid. p.13

can find such a match, it will use that prior solution as the model to drive this solution.

System One is a confident decision-maker, even when System Two steps in and corrects System One's error. When System One jumps in with a solution, it can make it harder for System Two to work out the right solution. For many people, that is exactly what happens in the basketball backboard and ball problem. They had to work harder than expected to get to the correct answer.

Here's how to easily solve the problem. Since the backboard is $100 more than the ball, if I gave you a discount of $100 for the backboard, then the ball and the backboard would cost the same amount.

So, the simple way to solve this problem is to take the total cost of the two items together ($110), subtract the difference between the two, ($100) leaving $10. Then divide the remainder ($10) by two, leaving the cost of the ball at $5. If you add the remaining amount ($5) back to the difference ($100) you get the cost of the pricier item, the backboard ($105). And it is correct because $105 is $100 more than $5.

If you want System One to get good at letting System Two solve this type of problem, then do the following five exercises in your head. By the time you solve the last one, you'll be good at it, and System One will not be interfering.

- Together, a tire and rim cost $200. The rim costs $150 more than the tire. How much does the tire cost?
- Together a small flashlight and battery cost $1.70. The flashlight costs $1.10 more than the battery. How much does the battery cost?
- As a set, a blazer and handkerchief cost $220. The blazer costs $200 more than the handkerchief. How much does the handkerchief cost?
- As a set, a desk and chair cost 300. The desk costs $200 more than the chair. How much does the chair cost?
- Together, a basketball backboard and ball cost $110. The backboard costs $100 more than the ball. How much does the ball cost?

Answers:
- The tire costs $25

- The battery costs $0.30
- The handkerchief costs $10
- The chair costs $50
- You already know this answer.

Ideally, in a sales situation you want to give System One the ability to make effortless decisions. But if your prospect employs the harder thinking of System Two, then you'd like him or her to come to the same decisions.

Science or Technology

In this book, I will include some of the science used to develop the Sales P.A.R. Excellence Strategy. But what is really at work here is technology.

What is the difference between pure science, and technology? One way to look at this is to think of technology as a tool that tells us "what" is happening and "how" to make it happen again. Science seeks to explain "why" all that is happening.

For example, charcoal burns hotter than wood even though it's made from wood. For eons, the extra heat charcoal gives off has enabled people to melt metals, which is why charcoal became a valuable commodity centuries ago. Many other technologies developed around this basic technology, such as controlling the air-flow (oxygen) to the charcoal fire, manufacturing charcoal to produce less waste, and using the waste to make briquettes.

It wasn't until recently that science could explain why charcoal burns hotter than wood. Simply put, when you burn wood a lot of energy is wasted vaporizing water and burning off other chemical components. By controlling the fire to burn everything but the carbon content of wood, you are left with charcoal.

When charcoal burns it is converted into CO_2, the pure burn of carbon in the charcoal produces more heat than the same mass of wood.

The important point for us is we did not need to know the science behind charcoal's effectiveness to make good use of it.

Likewise, we don't need science to make good use of the sales techniques in this book. However, understanding it enables us to use it more precisely as a technology, and perhaps gain other technological insights. Having said that, most of what I call 'the science' in this book is really the 'what and how' because we don't really have answers to 'why' things work in decision-making. As much as we have learned about the brain, a full understanding of the decision-making process is still out of reach.

I've based much of this book on the technology, we observe as 'working.' Why it works is, of course, both interesting and a subject of contemplation for psychologists and neuroscientists. The science attempts to explain 'what' our brains do in specific circumstances, which helps us understand 'how,' and perhaps a hint of 'why' the techniques work.

There are three overlapping fields of study useful in understanding the brain and human behavior. *Psychology* is the science of the mind, including human and animal behavior.

Behavioral Economics applies psychological insights to explain economic decision-making. The pioneers in behavioral economics were mostly psychologists, and most have interests in decision-making that extend well beyond economic decision-making.

Lastly, *Neuroscience* is the study of the brain and its inner workings. In this book's narrow focus, we will leverage neuroscience to provide understanding of what's going on in the brain when it is making economic decisions.

When developing the Sales P.A.R. Excellence Strategy, I relied heavily on synthesizing scientific studies to invent tools and subsequently field-test them to ensure their performance. While I am diligent in selecting which science is most reliable, it is useful to understand how reliable the science is overall, and how findings are concluded.

How Good is the Science?

The science around behavior is straightforward. We can observe behavior; we can do experiments, we can observe the results. Some of the behavior we observe we attribute to conscious decision-making. Other behavior we think derives from unconscious processes in the brain. Behavioral economics and psychology make conclusions based on the percentage of people's behavior that matches the expected outcome. Thus, the techniques here are based on predictive science that relies on probabilities.

For example, one study concludes that people evaluate an experience based on the remembered experience rather than the actual experience. This is based on the response of 22 out of 32 subjects in the trial. That's a very small sample size. What makes the science reliable is whenever you repeat the experiment the results are similar. Thus, the outcome is predictable for about 70 percent of people.

What takes place in decision-making is complex. How individuals respond to circumstances varies. A general relationship between cause and effect exists, but rarely does this work for 100 percent of people. This shortcoming shouldn't stop us from leveraging the insight.

I use a rule of thumb when reviewing psychology or behavioral economics. If there isn't a verifiable experiment showing a behavior occurring in context, it doesn't make the cut. There are many scientific papers in which a *theoretical psychologist* uses his or her insights to explain results without supplying experimental evidence to support the validity of the claim. Occasionally, biases significantly influence the work and result in poorly formed conclusions. For that reason, I leave those papers out of my research.

Neuroscience studies the brain itself, and what is taking place when different behaviors present themselves. In conducting research into the functioning of the brain, the scientists face some complex challenges.

Neuroscientists have a few main approaches for developing insights into the mind:

1. Someone suffers trauma to a specific part of their brain and loses (or gains) some observable function. When observed consistently in repeated instances of a trauma, that correlation implies causation[15].
2. Physiological instruments are used to measure biological activity. For example, the brain is imaged with fMRI (functional magnetic resonance imaging) to observe blood volume flow in the brain. Neuroscientists interpret increased blood flow in a specific part of the brain as that region connecting to the observed behavior.
3. With a probe, a targeted electric pulse is delivered to a specific spot in the brain and then correlated to a particular observed

---

[15] You will often hear people say, "Correlation doesn't prove causation." Which is true, because the correlation needs some plausibility. However, the only way to demonstrate plausible causation is through correlation. Correlation is all you see.

behavior. Scientist can also use the same probe technique to precisely measure electrical activity the brain itself generates[16].

4. Scientists perform a series of autopsies on brains of people who'd shared a characteristic or illness. The scientists compare the autopsies to 'normal' brains, and the differences linked to that characteristic.

However, "brain regions are typically engaged by many mental states, and thus a one-to-one mapping between a brain region and a mental state is not possible."[17] "For example, the amygdala is activated by arousal and positive emotions as well, so the key to interpreting such scans is a careful experimental design that allows comparison between brain states."[18] The

---

[16] Assuming the brain uses electrical activity to 'fire' neurons. They might actually be fired mechanically. See, Fox, Douglas. "The Brain, Reimagined." *Scientific American* 318.4 (2018): 60-67.

[17] NY Times, Letter to the Editor, "Politics and the Brain" from 17 PhD psychologist from the U.S. and Europe, NOV. 14, 2007, Opinion section in response to claims made in a Nov 11 2007 contribution entitled "This Is Your Brain on Politics".

[18] Shermer, Michael. "The Brain Is Not Modular: What

brain is a complex structure that has a constant hum of unconscious activity. The brain is regulating the heart, breathing, blinking, digesting, walking, and word formation, constantly watching for danger, along with hundreds of other subconscious activities. It is a busy organ, so when you're looking at brain activity, there is a lot of background noise. It is hard to separate all that unconscious activity from conscious activity.

Three other aspects add to the problem. First, it is never just one area of the brain that becomes more active during an observed behavior. It is difficult to show that one particular part is doing one particular thing.

Second, what takes place in the brain is very fast and complicated. If your measurement technique isn't as fast as the observed behavior or is out of sync, your conclusions will be questionable. For

---

FMRI Really Tells Us." *Scientific American*. N.p., 01 May 2008.

example, if you're studying what happens in the brain to trigger anger, you must rely on the person experiencing the anger to precisely report its time of onset. That's very hard to do for most humans.

Frequently, scientists examine the brain with an fMRI machine. The fMRI device measures the magnetic properties of blood oxygenation. In the brain, it can resolve to 1 mm^3, which contains between 12,000 and 15,000 neurons. It can resolve activity down to a temporal limit of 1 second. The problem is, a single neuron can fire 200 times per second, and can be connected to 1,000 other neurons. It's like shining a floodlight when what you need is a laser.

Brain probes allow for more precise observation, but neuroscientists don't risk healthy brains with that sort of invasive procedure. In neuroscience, "our understanding of the neural representation of different kinds of emotional reactions is still relatively limited."[19]

The third aspect is one of confusion. It happens when one group of psychologists will do an experiment, observe a phenomenon and give it a descriptive label. Another group will do a different kind of experiment and observe a very similar phenomenon and give it a completely different label.

For example, when we get to the discussion around the Intent Question, science says the *accessibility of the action* is the modulator for how influential the question is. Accessibility has to do with how vividly the brain sees an action. When we get to the discussion around the Counterfactual Hypothetical question, we see the same phenomenon, or at least a very similar phenomenon described as mental *elaboration*. Elaboration creates a vivid impression in the brain. Another study

---

[19] Phelps, Elizabeth A., Karolina M. Lempert, and Peter Sokol-Hessner. "Emotion and Decision Making: Multiple Modulatory Neural Circuits." Annual Review of Neuroscience 37.1 (2014): 263-87.

talks about how people tend to choose smaller immediate rewards over larger rewards received later on. This propensity leads to poor planning for retirement. But if you cause your subjects to enhance the *emotional salience* by "manipulating the mental representation of a future reward to make it more concrete,"[20] it will alter their behavior. There are three labels:

- accessibility,
- object of elaboration,
- emotional salience,

Each seems to describe the same fundamental phenomenon with a similar impact on decision-making. It is an example of what Albert Einstein said, "It is the theory that decides what we can observe."

The science opens up a world of deeper understanding that leads to tools we can use to improve our sales performance. As you've seen, the science isn't perfect. When

---

[20] Waugh, Christian E., J. Paul Hamilton, and Ian H. Gotlib. "The Neural Temporal Dynamics of the Intensity of Emotional Experience." *NeuroImage* 49.2 (2010): 1699-707.

it comes to understanding human decision making, there is more we don't know than we know. I encourage a little bit of skepticism, and don't be afraid to question the research, or my application of it.

A Question Is Worth A Thousand Statements.

The Sales P.A.R. Excellence strategy calls for asking three types of questions. We will focus on those three shortly. However, you can take practically any question you use today, and make it more influential to the listener by including a proposition. A proposition is a phrase or sentence that can be judged as either true or false.

For example, the question *"What time is it?"*

does not contain something that can be judged true or false. It has no propositional content. However, when the question is phrased a little differently— *"I've lost my Rolex, could you tell me what time it is?"* it contains a proposition that can be judged as either true or false— *'I've lost my Rolex.'*

Questions that contain a propositional component tend to pass more easily by the cognitive defenses of the listener.

After scientific investigators performed four experiments on how subjects process such questions, they found the cognitive impact was substantial. They concluded their study by recommending such questions be forbidden where influence is the objective[21].

A question is more or less influential by the ease with which the brain creates a mental

---

[21] Pandelaere, Mario, and Siegfried Dewitte. "Is This a Question? Not for Long. The Statement Bias." *Journal of Experimental Social Psychology*, vol. 42, no. 4, 2006, pp. 525–531.

representation of its propositional content. If you are going to ask an information-gathering question, add a propositional claim inside the question. For example, *"Sales P.A.R. Excellence strategy is proven to increase sales,"* is propositional content. It could pair with an information-gathering question such as— *"If you could increase production in your factory to meet an increase in demand, would you want your sales force to try to create that demand?"* Resulting in— *"If your factory could easily boost production to absorb an increase in sales, how strongly would you want your sales team to use a set of tools like Sales P.A.R. Excellence, that's proven to do exactly that?"*

How vividly the brain represents the proposition is determined by how easy the question is to understand, and the depth of processing required to answer it.

When processing a question, the brain converts the propositional content of the question, i.e. *"Sales P.A.R. Excellence tools enable you to increase your sales"* into a statement. Thus, it's remembered as a statement, not a question. That matters because the proposition is never challenged as either true or false. Remembering it as a statement increases its believability. This is particularly powerful when the same proposition is presented a second time.[22] It has become a familiar idea, which increases the proposition's credibility.

The goal of a sales call is to build cognitive impact. It is like adding power to a wave as it crosses the ocean. When the water is deep, the wave is almost imperceptible on the surface. When it reaches the shallow water of a coastline, the wave rises up and expends all the built up power as it breaks. Each influential question adds to the

---

[22] The callback is a technique used in stand-up comedy and by people adept at conversational humor. It is where the person includes a proposition early in the monologue and then returns to it in a slightly different way near or at the end. For some reason this tickles us. While I know of no science behind this, comedians say that the call-back works because the first instance allows the premise to become part of the listeners mental outlook and it sets up the premise as familiar so it has more punch the second time around, especially when it's included in a surprising way.

influential power in a sales call. You may not see it until it's decision time for the prospect.

To make this work for your sales efforts think through structuring your questions to include the propositional content you wish to communicate. When you do that, your questions can be influential while gathering information.

Answers make the heart grow fonder.

The questions discussed above can be influential independently of the answers. Starting with the next chapter it is the <u>answers</u> in which the cognitive impact is most powerful.

People tend to listen to themselves more than they do other people. In the movie Star Wars, Obi-Wan Kenobi waves his hand saying, "You don't need to see his identification." The stormtrooper says, "We don't need to see his identification." Obi-Wan then says, "These aren't the droids you're looking for." And the stormtrooper follows with, 'These aren't the droids we're looking for." Though this is from fiction, psychologically, it is when the stormtrooper spoke that the cognitive impact took hold.

The Peak/End Rule

How does deliberately increasing the amount of pain a patient feels in a colonoscopy lead to more effective sales to prospective clients?

We will start with the very last thing you do in your sales call. The Peak/End question is the easiest of the three question types to use. If you get nothing else from this book, you'll find this question is remarkably powerful. It is designed to provide the prospect with a lasting emotional connection to you.

This first psychological insight has to do with the emotional side of decision-making.

To achieve this, use the prospect's own answers. The answers will do triple duty for the sale. The prospect's answer will:
- Gather information for a follow-up note.
- Create an emotional peak.
- Cement a personal relationship.

Use a Peak/End question to end the sales call with an influential pleasant moment. Most great sales people will say it is the relationship that drives the sale. This Peak/End question cements that relationship.

Insight into this bit of psychology started when Gerry Kent published a finding that in dental procedures: "There was a closer association between remembered and expected pain than between remembered and experienced pain, particularly for those patients who scored high on the Dental Anxiety Scale."[23] Three months after people had their dental procedure, rather than remembering the pain they actually felt,

---

[23] Kent, Gerry. "Memory of Dental Pain." *Pain*, vol. 21, no. 2, 1985, pp. 187–194.

they remember the pain they'd expected before their procedure.

Then professor Ed Diener and his colleague David Thomas discovered that people who recorded their positive and negative moods across a day could not accurately report on their moods for the day as a whole[24]. They tended to overweigh negative emotions and under weigh the positive ones. The remembering self was different from the experiencing self. In the end, people are left with the remembering self.

Three years later, Dr. Donald Redelmeier and Professor Daniel Kahneman conducted a study in which patients recorded their discomfort level every sixty seconds during a colonoscopy.[25] Immediately after the procedure, and a month later the patients

---

[24] Thomas, D. L., & Diener, E. (1990). Memory accuracy in the recall of emotions. Journal of Personality and Social Psychology, 59, 291-297.
[25] Redelmeier, Donald, & Kahneman, Daniel. (1996). Patients' memories of painful medical treatments: Real-time and retrospective evaluations of two minimally invasive procedures. Pain. 66. 3-8. Written in 1993, (Note: Amos Tversky was Dr. Redelmeier's fellowship supervisor)

reported retrospectively on their overall pain experience. When looking at the worst moments and the final moments, one could reliably predict the patients remembered pain. Remarkably, the duration of the procedure (between 4 and 69 minutes) didn't have any effect on the remembered pain.

There is a fundamental belief in economics: people generally will choose what will cause most pleasure, and least pain. However, that choice is influenced by how we remember similar experiences. If memory is not accurate and is based on the most intense moments as well as the experience at the end, Kahneman next asked, could we be induced to make the irrational choice of more pain?

To get a more controlled environment Kahneman and his colleagues, Barbara Fredrickson, Charles Schreiber and Don Redelmeier, set up several of experiments to find this out. One of them I call 'the water torture'.[26]

They had test subjects immerse one of their hands in a plastic tub filled with seven liters of cold water (14°C) for 60 seconds. The subjects were not informed about the duration, they simply experienced it. During the 60 seconds the test subjects would periodically indicate on a 'discomfort meter' how much discomfort they felt on a scale of 0-14. After 60 seconds they dried off their hand and spent 7 minutes in a waiting area working on a personality inventory. Next, they were asked to put their other hand into the same temperature water. But this time, after the 60 seconds had passed they kept their hands immersed for 30 seconds longer as the temperature of the water was raised slightly. It was still cold enough to remain uncomfortable. Again, they dried off and had a 7 minutes wait. Next, the subjects

---

[26] Daniel Kahneman, Barbara L. Fredrickson, Charles A. Schreiber and Donald A. Redelmeier "When More Pain Is Preferred to Less: Adding a Better End." Psychological Science, vol. 4, no. 6, 1993, pp. 401–405.

were asked, "For today's third trial, you can pick one of the previous two cold-water trials. Which one do you choose?"[27]

Keep in mind that in both versions they experienced the same 60 seconds of pain, and in the second version they received an additional 30 seconds of pain. The duration of the two experiences was not pointed out to the subjects.

In analyzing the data, the subjects rated the initial 60 seconds of the two versions of the water torture the same at about 8.4 and 8.3 on a scale of 0-14. However, during the last 30 seconds of the longer trial the average of the 'discomfort meter' went down to 6.8 "still distinctly unpleasant"[28].

For their third water torture experience, 69 percent of the test subjects chose the longer version. However, not all test subjects had rated the final 30 seconds of the longer version the same way. Among those who

---

[27] Ibid, p. 402.
[28] Ibid, p. 403.

felt the biggest reduction in pain, over 80 percent chose the longer version with the same level of pain for the first 60 seconds, and a bit more pain for an additional 30 seconds. They willingly chose to endure more pain rather than less!

This experiment was repeated in various ways including with loud sounds, pleasant and unpleasant video clips, and as mentioned, colonoscopies. All these experiments showed the scientists that it is our faulty memory that determines our decisions and led Kahneman et al. to formulate the Peak/End Rule.

The Peak/End Rule applies to episodic experiences: those with a defined beginning, a consistent middle, and a defined ending. Your day, for example, has a defined beginning – you wake up, and a defined ending – you go to sleep. But the middle tends to be quite inconsistent. Lots of very different experiences happen during the day. Thus, the Peak/End Rule does not apply.

For a truly episodic experience, the Peak/End Rule states that the most intense moment, and the feeling at the end predict people's overall evaluation of the episode. Later research uncovered a strong impact of the <u>end</u> of an experience when that end is particularly meaningful.[29] The duration of the episode is mostly neglected.

The 'water torture' led to a second colonoscopy experiment. In agreeing to extend the discomfort of a colonoscopy for no medically necessary reason, the medical doctors were hoping to address a medical problem. The colonoscopy is a safe exam, highly effective in early detection of *colorectal* (colon) cancer. As people age, it is recommended they repeat this exam about every five years because, "One in 22 men and one in 24 women will be diagnosed with colorectal cancer in their

---

[29] Tully, Stephanie M., and Tom Meyvis. "Questioning the End Effect: Endings Do Not Inherently Have a Disproportionate Impact on Evaluations of Experiences." *SSRN Electronic Journal* (2014): n. pag.8

lifetime"[30].

The problem was, after their first painful colonoscopy experience, patients were likely to skip the next exam five years later. So, the doctors agreed that by applying the Peak/End Rule they might improve patients' memory of the experience and thus influence more of them to return in five years. This would improve the lives of some patients, so the doctors agreed to the experiment.

Dr. Donald Redelmeier is an internist currently affiliated with the Division of General Internal Medicine, Sunnybrook Health Sciences Centre, a teaching hospital of the University of Toronto Faculty of Medicine. He participated in the original colonoscopy experiment in which he and Kahneman monitored the level of pain during the procedure.

---

[30] "Colorectal Cancer Facts & Figures | Facts About Colon Cancer." *American Cancer Society*, www.cancer.org/research/cancer-facts-statistics/colorectal-cancer-facts-figures.html.

The colonoscopy is an episodic experience with a defined beginning, a consistent, but uncomfortable middle, and a defined end. From patients' perspective, the colonoscopy exam ends when the instrument is removed from their body. So, the natural application of the Peak/End Rule would be, after the normal exam was concluded, to leave the instrument laying unmoved inside the patient for a short period of time. This added experience was mildly uncomfortable, but for many patients it would be much less painful than the preceding moments during the exam. It would make for a different ending, therefore a differently remembered experience.[31]

In all, 682 colonoscopy patients volunteered to participate in this blind experiment. Half the patients were

---

[31] This would be a difficult study to do today because most colonoscopies are now done with the patient given a drug combination like Versed/Fentanyl/Propofol or Versed/Fentanyl/Demerol where there is diminished experienced pain and often no memory of pain or the procedure at all.

randomly selected to get a regular colonoscopy, while the other half would have the colonoscope left in place for about a minute after the medical exam was completed. The 'experiencing' patients would have preferred the uncomfortable instrument be removed earlier. For many of the patients, this added minute was a much less painful experience than the preceding medical exam.

The researchers let six years pass and examined return rates for the two groups. When accounting for the patient's prior history or abnormal findings, the longer test procedure showed a 41 percent increase in the odds of the patient returning for a subsequent colonoscopy.[32]

Barbara L. Fredrickson, a key researcher in the water torture study, argues that peaks and ends earn their privileged status because they carry more personal meaning

---

[32] Redelmeier, Donald A, et al. "Memories of Colonoscopy: a Randomized Trial." *Pain*, vol. 104, no. 1, 2003, pp. 187–194.

than other moments[33]. This insight is baked into the strategy in the *Peak Interview*, which formed the testing ground for the Sales P.A.R. Excellence approach. Simply put, if you can combine the most intense Peak with the End, you double up on their power to influence. If you also ensure that there is a great deal of personal meaning in the moment you've maximized the effect it has on how someone judges the quality of the episode (such as reflecting on the candidate in a job interview, or the salesperson in a sale).

The Peak/End Question

The sales call is an episodic experience. It has a defined beginning, a pretty consistent middle, and a defined ending. You want to create an end peak that works well for building a relationship with the prospect. A strong peak at the end will color the prospect's memory for how good the

---

[33] Fredrickson, Barbara L. "Extracting Meaning from Past Affective Experiences: The Importance of Peaks, Ends, and Specific Emotions." *Cognition & Emotion*, vol. 14, no. 4, 2000, pp. 577–606.

experience was.

In an effort to combine the most intense peak moment with the ending, while making it personally meaningful, we've formulated the Peak/End Question. Remember, the buyer needs to experience the peak while speaking because the act of talking stimulates the brain and the subconscious more than listening. The more active the brain, the more powerful is the influence.

The Peak Sale tactic ends the conversation with your prospect by asking a question along the lines of: *"It has been fascinating talking with you. I suspect you've had some very interesting experiences along the way. Looking back over your career, what the one thing you've done that you're most proud of?"*

Why this question? We are trying to activate the prospect's brain, particularly the emotional centers of the brain. In a study reported by Diana Tamir and Jason Mitchell at Harvard, participants were asked to talk about their own beliefs and opinions and to speculate about those of another person while undergoing fMRI monitoring. The study showed the areas of the brain associated with pleasure and reward were activated more strongly when the participants were talking about themselves, than when they were talking about the other person.[34]

It's well known that people love to talk about themselves. Perhaps that's why upwards of 80 percent of posts to social media consist of reporting your own personal experiences. Now, there's science to prove it.

Over the past seven years, this Peak/End question has been used thousands of times. People will answer this question. Your job is to be quiet and listen. The prospect may start with one story and switch to another.

---

[34] Tamir, D. I., and J. P. Mitchell. "Disclosing Information about the Self Is Intrinsically Rewarding." *Proceedings of the National Academy of Sciences* 109.21 (2012): 8038-043.

People love to talk, particularly around action they are proud of. Your job is to just listen and encourage. When they are finished, so is the sales call. This is absolutely the key. Any house keeping, such as setting up a follow-up sales call or promising to send information must be done before asking the Peak/End question. When the prospect is finished answering the Peak/End question, thank the prospect and leave.

This Peak/End leaves prospects with a good feeling that the time spent with the sales person was worthwhile. It creates a good bond between the salesperson and the prospect. Then, when following up the sales call with a thank you note, mention the story the prospect told and say you'd love to hear more next time. The prospect will remember you and briefly relive the peak experience.

Question Of Intent

Behavioral economists and psychologists have shown that merely getting someone to tell you their intent to do something will increase the probability that they will actually do it.

Fall had begun at Ohio State University and it was a couple of days before the voter registration deadline. Phone calls were made to 416 students in the dormitories of the university[35]. It turned out that a

---

[35] Greenwald, Anthony G., Catherine G. Carnot, Rebecca Beach, and Barbara Young. "Increasing Voting Behavior by Asking People If They Expect to Vote." *Journal of Applied Psychology* 72.2 (1987): 315-18

majority of students understood their civic duty and were already registered to vote. Those who were not registered were asked if they would participate in a study. Most readily agreed. The study ended up with 62 unregistered voters for the research. All 62 students received a phone call and were asked a series of voter knowledge questions including if they knew of the registration deadline and where to register.

Then, through a random selection process, 32 of the students were asked a 'prediction' question, "What do you expect to do between now and the registration deadline of Tuesday evening? Do you expect that you will register to vote or not?" Those students who indicated they intended to register were asked this further question, "What would you say is the most important single reason for your registering to vote?" The other 30 students did not get either of these questions.

After the elections, publicly available voter registration records were examined and follow-up calls were made to the students.

The result showed students who were asked the intent question were more than twice as likely to have actually registered to vote than the students who were not asked this question.

The psychology department performed a second study with a different group of students the day before the presidential elections. Out of this group half were asked their intention to vote the next day, half were not. As in the prior experiment, a significantly higher percent voted when asked the intent question (87 percent) versus no intent question (62 percent).

Studies of intent questions could have stopped with the simply insight that asking an intent question increases the likelihood of a person taking the action. But then the researcher stumbled upon something unexpected.

In a large study, thousands of people were asked their intention to buy a car in the next few months. People who were asked this question bought more cars than the control group[36]. Then, researchers noticed that people who already owned a particular brand of car were more likely to buy that brand, and people who did not own a car were more likely to buy from a more heavily advertised brand in their local area.

This led scientists Jonathan Levav and Gavin Fitzsimons[37] to hypothesize that when asking an intent question, the likelihood of resulting behavior is increased by how easily the subject can mentally imagine it. Levav and Fitzsimons decided to conduct a series of experiments.

They divided 99 students into four groups, A, B, C, and D. All students answered a ten question "market research survey" about various food consumption habits. In addition:

---

[36] Fitzsimons, Gavan J., and Vicki G. Morwitz. "The Effect of Measuring Intent on Brand-Level Purchase Behavior." *Journal of Consumer Research* 23.1 (1996)

[37] Levav, Jonathan, and Gavan J. Fitzsimons. "When Questions Change Behavior." *Psychological Science* 17.3 (2006): 207-13. Gavan prepared this for a talk in Chicago and the U of C Graduate School of Business (now Booth).

- 23 students in group A were asked to indicate the likelihood they would consume fatty foods during the coming week.
- 25 students in group B were asked to indicate the likelihood they would not consume fatty foods during the coming week.
- 26 students in group C were asked to indicate the likelihood they would avoid consuming fatty foods during the coming week.
- 25 students in group D were asked to indicate the likelihood they would consume orange drinks during the coming week. (The control group)

All four groups then participated in an hour of unrelated experiments to take their minds off this intent question.

Their final task was a taste test. They could choose one of two foods to consume as part of the taste test, either a rice cake (not fatty), or a chocolate chip cookie (fatty).

92 percent of the control group (group D who got the juice question) chose the cookie - they were college kids! In group A, 65 percent of chose the cookie, as did 68 percent of group B. The word 'fatty' is a

negative adjective. The researchers expected that using it within a question of the intent to eat something would reduce the likelihood someone would eat food deemed 'fatty'. The psychologists pointed out that the idea of not eating something is hard to imagine without imagining eating it. So groups A and B should have behaved similarly. Thus, by simply raising a question about eating 'fatty' foods, caused students to eat fewer cookies as expected.

Group C had been asked about their intent to <u>avoid</u> fatty foods. Group C students were able to imagine distinct behaviors of avoiding eating fatty foods. This made the action more vivid and the intent question that much more powerful. Only 38 percent of Group C chose the cookie.

If you want to influence a behavior, ask the prospect's intent to do it, but make the behavior easy to represent mentally. The more vivid, the better.

Attention and Intention

For example, as part of the discovery process you can ask an intent question, *'What is the likelihood you will make a purchase decision today?'*–when answered the likelihood of the action happening increases. In fact, if you find out something about the purchasing decision process, you can increase the cognitive impact of an intent question by making the action you're asking about easy for the prospect to imagine.

Formulate intent questions to meet your unique discovery needs, for example:

"Is it your intention to make a purchase recommendation to senior management?"

Or you could make the action more accessible.

"At the end of this process, after talking to sales people like me, is it your intention to put together a document of the pro's and con's of the alternatives, rank the options by your company's needs, and make an intelligent and well supported

recommendation to senior management?"

Alternatively, you could boost the power of the question by incorporating into the query a Counterfactual Hypothetical (which we'll cover shortly).

"Looking ahead, now this isn't true, at least not yet, but imagine for the sake of understanding your process, after reviewing the alternatives let's say my company's solution was the best fit. Would it be your intention to get as much support as you can from me and my team to enable you to present a very strong and well documented recommendation to senior management to purchase our solution?"

Questions work when they are comfortable to ask and relevant to the current sale. You want to ask questions when you feel confident the questions will be answered.

The objective here isn't to give you a defined set of intent questions. You should make your own questions. The sales and leadership teams can get together and formulate a handful of intent questions specific to the products and services your sell, and then build-up those questions to be as influential as possible.

Beauty in the eyes of the responder.

The real power of an intent question is not found in the question, it's found in the answer. It is what your prospects say that is most influential to them. In the end, it is always ourselves we listen to most.

The next chapter studies using the Counterfactual Hypothetical question. The answer to a properly formed Counterfactual Hypothetical question is an extraordinarily powerful source of cognitive impact. It has closed the deal for many readers of The Peak Interview because it addresses both the emotional and rational components of decision-making.

The Counterfactual Hypothetical

On the internet you can find lists of the best open-ended questions to use on a sales call. One such question is: *"If you were suddenly transported three years into the future, how will all this look different?"* It is a Counterfactual Hypothetical question (meaning it's not true – counterfactual; and a 'what if' - hypothetical scenario). However, this particular Counterfactual Hypothetical question is not well crafted for cognitive impact. One can learn how to do much better.

The Counterfactual Hypothetical question

is a powerful sales tool. It will influence what people think and can change people's behavior.

This type of question does three important things in a sales situation. First, it is natural for the buyer to have their cognitive defenses on high alert during a sales call. A properly constructed Counterfactual Hypothetical question will soften the cognitive defenses of the prospect. That's because the question does not sound like an attempt to influence. If it is clear to the listener that what is said is intended to influence, then his or her cognitive defenses are alerted and the ability to influence is greatly reduced[38].

The Counterfactual Hypothetical is structured so it does not turn on the person's cognitive defenses because no truth claim is made. Often a Counterfactual Hypothetical is prefaced with, "This isn't

---

[38] Patti Williams; Gavan J Fitzsimons; Lauren G Block, "When Consumers Do Not Recognize "Benign" Intention Questions as Persuasion Attempts", *Journal of Consumer Research;* Dec 2004; 31, 3; l pg. 540

true, but image if..."

The second important thing a Counterfactual Hypothetical question does, is to get the prospect talking. The action of talking triggers emotional centers in the brain. The more active the emotional centers are, the better. The emotional centers in the brain are where choices are made. Many people have experienced a time when they needed to talk about something with deep personal meaning for them. They can go over what they plan to say in their heads, but the instant they start to talk about it, they feel themselves loosing control of their emotions.

Lastly, we are delivering a message. Every day we have conversations with others in which it's clear we're not getting through. It might be that we are doing a poor job on our end of the conversation. Or it could be that our listener, lost in thought, is just not hearing us. By allowing our message to be constructed while the prospect is doing the talking, we know it's getting through.

The classic example of the behavioral influence of the Counterfactual Hypothetical is the work done by Gavan Fitzsimons and Baba Shiv. They found, *"that even though such questions are purely hypothetical, respondents are unable to prevent a substantial biasing effect on their behavior."*[39]

Three hundred and seventy-seven undergraduate students participated in a two-part study. One part was about the effects of a change in environment on how consumers express opinions about products (a disguise for the real study). The students were told they would be provided with a choice of snacks for participating in the study. In the other part of the study, they were given a set of questions to answer, including hypothetical questions.

Participants in both the control groups and the test groups were asked to estimate how

---

[39] Fitzsimons, Gavan J., and Baba Shiv. "Non-conscious and Contaminative Effects of Hypothetical Questions on Subsequent Decision Making." *Journal of Consumer Research* 28.2 (2001): p.224

many times a month they consume cakes, pastries, and so forth. The test group got this further question, *"If strong evidence emerges from scientific studies suggesting that cakes, pastries, etc. are not nearly as bad for your health as they have often been portrayed to be, and may have major health benefits, what would happen to your consumption of these items? Please think carefully before you respond to the question. You will be asked to justify your response later."*[40]

They next spent an hour performing the other part of the study, the disguise part. Afterward, as they walked to the second room of the experiment, they were given a choice of two snacks — a piece of chocolate cake or a serving of fruit salad.

The researches then asked the study participants if they believed the hypothetical about cakes having major health benefits was true. All of the students in the test group said they knew it wasn't

---

[40] Ibid 230-231

true. Nevertheless, among the students who were asked the hypothetical question suggesting cake was healthy, 66 percent chose the cake, while only 25 percent of the control group took the cake.

Just answering the Counterfactual Hypothetical question about cakes influenced their choice of cake. The next question for the researchers was, what mediates and moderates this behavior, what is it that makes this question work?

One thing Gavan Fitzsimons and Baba Shiv tested in their study was relevance. To test this idea, they posed two versions of the cake question to different groups of students. In the high relevance version, the Counterfactual Hypothetical suggested cakes have "major health benefits." Sixty-six percent of subjects in the high relevance group took the cake. In the low relevance condition, the cakes have "minor health benefits" and 36 percent of participants took the cake (slightly more than the control group at 25 percent). The Counterfactual Hypothetical question is more influential on subsequent behavior when the question is relevant.

Then, Sarah Moore, and David Neal, joined Gavan Fitzsimons and Baba Shiv to further investigated how and when hypothetical questions influence individuals.[41]

They discovered the key to the power of the question was elaboration. Elaboration is the amount of thinking or talking a person does in answering the Counterfactual Hypothetical. They used the same set-up as for the health benefits of eating cake. The control group did not get the Counterfactual Hypothetical question and they again chose cake 25 percent of the time. The test group consisted of two subgroups, the low elaboration group and the high elaboration group. The high elaboration subgroup received an additional instruction: *"Please think*

---

[41] Moore, Sarah G., David T. Neal, Gavan J. Fitzsimons, and Baba Shiv. "Wolves in Sheep's Clothing: How and When Hypothetical Questions Influence Behavior." *Organizational Behavior and Human Decision Processes* 117.1 (2012): 168-78.

carefully before you respond to the question. You will be asked to justify your response later." While subjects in the low elaboration subgroup, got the Counterfactual Hypothetical question without the added instruction.

The low elaboration subgroup's behavior was still changed by the Counterfactual Hypothetical question; 45.5 percent of them took the cake. The high elaboration group (where they were told *"You will be asked to justify your response later"*) took more cake: 69 percent. They concluded if you want a Counterfactual Hypothetical answer to have more cognitive impact, then cause the person answering the question to experience more elaboration.

This and other experiments using the same techniques measured two features of the question: relevance and elaboration. The more relevant a question is and the more elaboration required in answering the question, the more powerful the cognitive impact of the question is on subsequent decision-making.

OUTSELL

In The Peak Interview I included a Counterfactual Hypothetical question:

"Lets say, it's now a year into the job, we're going over my annual performance review, and say, I've had a truly outstanding year, I did everything you expected, wished for and more, what have I accomplished in this first year?"

The question the hiring manager hears comes down to, "what makes for outstanding performance?" Any hiring manager worth their salt knows they should answer it. It is highly relevant to the interview and requires a great deal of elaboration. We've had thousands of job applicants use this question to great effect. They attribute their success in getting the job offer to this question and to the Peak/End question (which we discussed earlier in this book).

Human decision-making has an emotional component and a rational component. The Counterfactual Hypothetical question covers both. You will craft your own Counterfactual Hypothetical question, and it should be very similar to this one:

"Now, this isn't true, but imagine you bought our solution and it turned out to be just exactly the right one for you and your company. It's now a year later and it's been an outstanding year. What have you accomplished in this year as a result of buying our solution?"

Some salespeople will say, *"Hold on, isn't it my job to lay this out for the prospect, to paint the picture of what it's going to look like after they buy from me?"* No. It's an approach you will find in some books on selling, but it doesn't have the desired impact the way the Counterfactual Hypothetical question does. The Counterfactual Hypothetical question causes prospects to paint this picture themselves. Remember, you're better able to create cognitive impact in the prospect when the prospect is doing the talking.

I say 'a question very similar to this one'

because you are going to make it your own question. What is critical in constructing this question is:
- It is not true (yet)
- It's a 'what if' question
- It involves you, your company, and your organization.

The absolute wrong way to ask this is: "*but imagine you bought a solution from the ideal company*". The prospect will then talk about some ideal company, not you!

Why is that so important? The Counterfactual Hypothetical has the magic quality of both operating at a conscious level where the person answering the question knows it's not true, while at the same time, operating at the unconscious level, where the subconscious forgets that it's not true, and begins to attribute the capability to deliver these good outcomes to you.

The other important aspect of the question is it removes a key cognitive barrier. For example, walking into a warehouse-size electronics store, a salesperson in a store uniform asks, "Can I help you?" Immediately your cognitive defenses kick into gear, and your reflexive response is, "No thank you, I'm just browsing."

With cognitive defenses up, the prospect will look for opportunities to mentally pick apart what you say. Those defenses cause our brains to engage in <u>active</u> rational thinking about what might <u>not</u> be true. However, when starting your Counterfactual Hypothetical question with "Now, this isn't true, but imagine…" immediately, the prospect lets down those cognitive defenses. The 'facts' you put on the table have been established as untrue. When answering a question like this, prospects are not defending anything.

After establishing the upcoming situation is not true, we let the prospect take us into an imaginary world. It's the one in which purchasing our product or service has turned out great for both our prospect and his or her company. Any salesperson would love to control that narrative.

Setting up the answer to the Counterfactual Hypothetical question

We can't actually control the story entirely. However, the goal is to ensure we place our prospect in the position of constructing the right response.

Before asking the Counterfactual Hypothetical, set it up in a way that gives the prospect both: an emotional trigger to activate the choice engine in the emotional centers of the brain; and rational reasons that will support a buying decision down the road.

Next, we want to reduce the appearance of risk our prospect feels in making a buying decision. If you're selling to the CEO/Owner of the business, it will be easier when it comes to the risk question. For all other prospects, one of their big risks is personal, "what will happen to me if this turns out badly?" CEO/Owners don't worry about this at a personal level.

For example, take the purchasing manager

whom the CEO/Owner has assigned to select an enterprise network solutions provider. A Request-For-Proposal (RFP) is prepared with the IT department, and sent out to a dozen companies. Responses come back from companies like Cisco of San Jose, CA., Ekulf Network Solutions in Latvia, Tulosten in Korea[42], among others. It turns out that the company that best matched the requirements of the RFP was Ekulf Network Solutions. So which network provider does the purchasing manager select?

Cisco, of course!

The purchasing manager is sure the CEO has heard of Cisco, after all it controls 60 percent of the market. But, it's unlikely the CEO or any senior manager has heard of Ekulf or Tulosten. If something goes badly wrong with the new network and the purchasing manager chose Ekulf, the blame falls on the purchasing manager. If it's Cisco, who is blamed? Cisco!

---

[42] Tulosten and Ekulf are fictitious names.

We want a story that takes away personal risk for the prospect.

We also want to find a way to let the prospect feel a personal benefit from choosing our product. Ideally, we want the prospect to feel as though they might just become the company hero for bringing in our solution. The prospect should also acquire a vision of enhanced identity and meaning from making this purchase decision[43].

The four components that set-up the Counterfactual Hypothetical question are:
- Emotional triggers
- Rational reasons
- Removing risks
- Making heroes

The first component is the emotional

---

[43] "Identity" in this context is how we want others to see us. It is dependent upon others. "Meaning" is purely personal. It doesn't really matter if what's meaningful to me is not meaningful to others.

trigger. The typical businessperson doesn't believe he or she makes the buying decision by engaging the emotional centers of the brain. It isn't just a denial. People firmly believe they make a business decision on purely rational bases. In fact, people will argue it was purely a rational decision, without emotional influence.

Neuroscientists might argue that decision-making without emotional influence is not possible. Damage to the ventromedial sector in the brain affects social behavior and decision-making. Most other intellectual capabilities are maintained. They have normal memory and learning ability. They maintain normal language function and normal attention. They even perform well in executive function tests. However, the damage prevents these people from engaging their emotions in relation to complex situations and events. For example, in situations where they should feel the emotion of embarrassment, they don't. The emotional engine is impaired.

When executing a test of repeated decision-making with good and bad outcomes, people without brain damage quickly learn to avoid the bad decisions. However, people with damage to the ventromedial sector are unable to process the emotion of bad decisions and do not learn to avoid them even with repeated trials. Their decision engine is impaired.[44]

The truth is we don't know exactly what is going on in the brain when a decision is made. We just know it involves the emotional centers of the brain and emotions activate that choice center.

Moreover, evidence is strong that decisions are made subconsciously. In fact, experiments show telltale brain activity of subjects before they make a conscious decision. In some experiments the researchers could predict, based on specific brain activity, what decision the subject

---

[44] Bechara, A, et al. "Emotion, Decision Making and the Orbitofrontal Cortex." *Cerebral Cortex (New York, N.Y. : 1991).*, U.S. National Library of Medicine, Mar. 2000.

would make, before the subjects had made the decision.[45] Scary stuff!

At the same time, the prospect's brain should have a rational basis for the decision. When the prospect answers the Counterfactual Hypothetical question, he or she will be constructing a rationale to support a subsequent purchase decision. To accomplish that, enhance the impact of this rational side by making it more emotionally important for the buyer.

Essentially, let the buyer describe the wonderful impact of buying your product or service in a way that makes the buyer feel that impact. Set up that narrative with a story or two.

The story gives the prospect some elements of the rational reason for making the buy decision. When I work with companies, one

---

[45] Soon, Chun Siong, Marcel Brass, Hans-Jochen Heinze, and John-Dylan Haynes. "Unconscious Determinants of Free Decisions in the Human Brain." *Nature Neuroscience* 11.5 (2008): 543-45

of the first things the leadership team does[46] is a short exercise to articulate the company's value proposition(s). These are the reasons customers buy the company's products or services.

The exercise starts with team members writing down the company's value proposition as they see it. I remind them to include only features and benefits relevant to the customer. In spite of the instruction, the value propositions written always include features the company is proud of (such as the number of patents they hold or the number of decades the company has existed), on the assumption that if it matters internally, it must matter to customers.

A fun outcome of this exercise is that no two answers are the same. Directionally, they are typically consistent.

---

[46] It may seem odd that I work with the leadership team to create the strategy and stories we use in the Sales P.A.R. Excellence strategy. I find that the different personality types and the different perspectives you get from the leadership team makes the outcome far richer than if you just used the sales team.

Sometimes you get something that's very different from the rest. At first it sounds like it came out of left field, but then you see nodding heads around the table.

Using the different perspectives, the team creates a straw-man value proposition. Then, I challenge them on every part of it. How do we verify these are key for the customer?

At that point, I mention two books. One is by my favorite physicist, Richard Feynman. Among physicists, he is often considered the most important physicist of the 20th century (including Albert Einstein). Feynman wrote a book entitled "What do you care what other people think?"[47] What matters in physics, isn't what people think, e.g. "we think the world is flat", but rather, what is demonstrably true (can be tested to be false). Opinions don't matter. Likewise, the opinions of team members about the

---

[47] This Feynman book was preceded by one entitled: *Surely You're Joking, Mr. Feynman!*

customer fall into this category. It is what the customer really thinks that matters.

The second book is a wonderful marketing book called 'Tuned In' by Craig Stull, Phil Myers, and David Meerman Scott. The most famous phrase from that book is: "Your opinion, although interesting, is irrelevant." Your internally created value propositions for products and services fall into that category. Interesting, but irrelevant.

Well, only partly irrelevant because at this point it is all a salesperson has. What matters most is what's going on in the prospect's head. What does the prospect see as the value proposition? That is why I challenge the leadership team. They should feel that they are pretty close to what the customer thinks. We want to seed the prospect's brain with a story that addresses the relevant key benefit.

The value proposition attempts to identify which benefits matter to the customer. Then the leadership team identifies the features of the product or service most relevant to delivering those sought-after benefits to the customer. The features must differentiate us from the competition. A long list of features is produced because the team thinks the company does lots of things better than the competition.

At this point the team has two lists; a list of benefits, and a list of product features that deliver the benefits.

They then pick a representative customer and rank the benefits from the perspective of that customer. For the top benefit they then prioritize the relevant features.

Every salesperson suffers from knowing the company's products and service really well. Many would want to share this wealth of knowledge with the prospect. However, psychologists tell us that with too many choices, the customer is more likely to choose nothing at all, and with too much information, the customer feels overwhelmed and confused and doesn't absorb anything of value[48].

This is where it gets hard for the leadership team because they must select one, and only one, feature to talk about[49]. They must be able to explain how that feature produces differentiation from the competition.

The next exercise requires the team to identify customer cases in which the identified feature supported the chosen benefit. For each case, a member of the team will lay out the story. After ranking the quality of the stories, choose one to be developed for the sales team.

This story is about what the prospect's company stands to <u>gain</u> from buying our

---

[48] Iyengar, Sheena S., and Mark R. Lepper. "When Choice Is Demotivating: Can One Desire Too Much of a Good Thing?" *Journal of Personality and Social Psychology* 79.6 (2000): 995-1006.

[49] Eventually you are going to create a handful of stories around a set of key benefits and features, which will allow the salesperson to pull out the right story for the right prospect. Also, in the story it is okay to drop a comment about another feature as long as you don't change the focus on just one main feature.

product or service.

Risk matters most

Perhaps even more important is a story that includes the risk. The objective is to reduce or eliminate the sense of personal risk felt by our prospect.

Behavioral economists have investigated the balance between gain and loss.[50] Think about finding a $20 bill on the sidewalk. Pick it up, look around to see if there is a likely rightful owner, and seeing none, pocket the windfall. You feel fortunate. You keep it in your pocket for a couple of days and don't think much more about it. Then on the third day, reaching into your pocket to pull out your $20, it's not there. You ponder when you last had it. You feel certain it was in your pocket this morning. Where could it have gone? You've lost it. You will worry about this for far longer and with greater energy than you gained by

---

[50] This is well covered in a book I recommend every business leader read: Thinking Fast and Slow, by Daniel Kahneman.

finding the $20 in the first place. In financial accounting terms the net is zero. In emotional terms the net is a significant minus. It may bother you for more than a couple of days. The loss will more than offset the pleasure you enjoyed earlier of finding the $20.

Loss is more intense than gain, and the fear of loss is more exaggerated than the feeling of opportunity for gain. The gain story around features and benefits will provide the prospect with the rational reason for buying the product. A story that reduces perceived risk for the prospect will address the emotional component of the purchase. The best stories have the risk resolution baked into the narrative, which is resolved at the end of the story.

In a business-to-business transaction, where the prospect is not the CEO or Owner, anticipate that your prospect has a fear of personal loss.

One key element in the set-up to the Counterfactual Hypothetical question is dealing with the prospect's risk. Having mentioned the <u>personal</u> risk the prospect likely faces, the prospect may surface other <u>business</u> risks, such as:

- Technology change
- Engineering quality
- Missed delivery dates
- Safety
- The market will be disrupted
- Internal dissention
- Product will fail
- New materials will come out that change the economics
- The company is late to the game
- As first adopters, too early to the game
- Poor support after the sale
- Choose the wrong brand
- Something important is overlooked
- Lack of knowledge
- And probably a dozen more.

Then, there are plenty of uncontrollable risks – political risk, state of the economy, war, natural disasters, etc.

In a workshop to build the Sales P.A.R. Excellence Strategy for a company, we do an exercise that enables us to identify the likely risks buyers face, and prioritize them.

With this list, it is time to develop stories that deal with the key risks.

In the sales call, the discovery process will include trying to identify which risk is key for this prospect. Don't expect the prospect to be too forthcoming. A salesperson will likely have to use some intuition to identify the risk and tell a story which addresses it.

For example, the selling company is SlurryThermal Inc.[51] It makes equipment for direct steam technology used for inline food cooking and similar applications. It has new technology with a more cost effective way to heat foods than older heat exchangers or kettle cookers along with a handful of other excellent features.

About 65 percent of SlurryThermal customers list innovation as one of their core values.

The SlurryThermal team has identified

---

[51] This is a fictitious company.

deep cleaning time as a key feature. The cleanup time can be as fast as ten minutes as compared to taking an entire eight hour shift for a deep cleaning of a kettle cooker. Between batches of a single product their cooker can self clean in less than a minute.

To support the innovation benefit, they came up with the following story.

In a sales call, the salesperson has already discovered innovation is a key activity in this prospect's company. The salesperson then asks the purchasing manager, "If you had to pick out one feature of a modern cooker that's very important to your company, what would come to mind right away?"

The prospect says, "Well, that's easy. With our kettle cookers, we bring down the production line for a whole shift once a week to clean them. A cooker with a faster cleanup time is key. It would allow us to be more productive." At this point, the salesperson knows which story to use, that will help to set-up the Counterfactual

OUTSELL

Hypothetical question the salesperson will ask later. The story is there to provide narrative elements the prospect can use later in answering the Counterfactual Hypothetical.

"Well," replies the salesperson. "That's a good reason to look at our cooker. It does clean up fast, which can increase your innovation. In fact, that reminds me of something funny that happened a couple of weeks ago to one of my colleagues, Pat."

"Pat got a call from a pretty angry purchasing manager. Their company had installed one of our cookers about six months ago."

"The purchasing manager was agitated. He said to Pat. 'Our finance chief just left my office. Guess what, he showed me operations data that your cooker is down for cleaning for eight hours every week, just like our kettle cookers. You promised me a ten-minute cleanup time. I'm looking like an idiot here!' Pat was surprised."

" 'That's very odd. Listen, I'll be in your neighborhood this afternoon, could I stop by and take a look? Something must be wrong.' "

" 'You bet something is wrong, and it better be fixed. By all means, come by this afternoon.' "

"So later that afternoon Pat and the purchasing manager are in the plant, there's a loud hum of activity and the company is cooking something that smells delicious. They're looking at the cooker, and poor Pat can't find anything wrong. He's standing there scratching his head; with the purchasing manager standing hands on hips glaring at him. Just then the CEO walks by. Apparently he is a walk-around manager, and he sees Pat scratching his head, walks over and asks what's going on."

"Pat shakes his head, 'We have a problem, and I'm at a loss to explain it.' "

" 'Well what's the problem?' Asks the CEO."

"The purchasing manager jumps in. 'We're supposed to be seeing a weekly deep cleaning of ten minutes, instead it's taking eight hours, it's as bad as our kettle cookers!' "

"The CEO looks startled and asks 'Who told you that?' "

" 'Our CFO. It's on the production reports,' answered the purchasing manager."

" 'Ah, well we better fix the reports,' Laughed the CEO. 'So, to clear this up, there isn't a problem with the cleanup.' He looks at Pat and says, 'You cooker deep cleans in no time at all, and better still, it self-cleans between batches in less than a minute.' "

"The CEO took a breath, 'Look, here is the thing. I have a staff of four food scientists who are constantly itching to test new products. It is almost impossible to get test-time in one of our big kettles and it turns out that something that works great on the test-bench in the lab often doesn't turn out the same in the big kettles,' the CEO smiled, 'So when the rest of the production line is down for cleaning we use your cooker to test these scientists' ideas. We can do upwards of twenty to thirty different tests in that window of time. Did you know we're able control the temperature to within less than a degree even when we change the flow rate, the slurry density, or the pressure in the system? It's incredible. In fact, since we installed this cooker,' the CEO put his hand out and patted the cold-flow pipe, 'we have eleven new products in final flavor testing and will launch them later this year. That's already three times as many as we did all last year and we're only five months into the year,' the CEO grinned approvingly and looked over at the purchasing manager, 'so, no we don't have a problem and I apologize because I've been meaning to stop by your office and thank you for talking us into buying this cooker. It has been such a surprise, it's perfect!' "

"You can imagine how relieved Pat was. And as far as I know it's the only time anyone has had a, 'problem', even an imaginary one, with the cleanup time of our cookers".

The example story is fictional. Yours will be a true story.

Earlier I listed four components to build-up before asking the Counterfactual Hypothetical.
- Emotional triggers
- Rational reasons
- Removing risks
- Making heroes

In the above example the prospect listening to the story is the purchasing manager. At the end of the story, the purchasing manager is the hero in the eyes of the CEO. We don't have to say it explicitly because we can safely assume our prospect empathizes with the purchasing manager in the story and will feel how great it is to get a compliment from the CEO. That's our emotional trigger.

The story also delivers the rational reasons for the purchase:

- Increases innovation.
- Cleans up faster.
- Incredible temperature control.
- Adjusts to changes on the fly, such as slurry density, flow rate, and pressure.
That is the rational reason.

The resolution of the 'long cleanup time problem' is there to remove the risk, and the pat-on-the-back by the CEO is to 'make a hero' of the purchasing manager.

Later, the salesperson will ask the Counterfactual Hypothetical: "Now, this isn't true, but imagine you bought our product (service) and it turned out to be just exactly the right solution for you and your company. It's now a year later and it's been an outstanding year. What have we enabled you to accomplish in this year?" The prospect can pull ideas from the earlier story, and perhaps one or two more from stories you've told, to describe how the year turned out so well. Our stories seed this answer.

When you make claims about your product in a story they are more credible than if you just came out and made the claim, "some customers think our cookers are perfect." The claim just isn't as credible. The story changes that perspective, because it's the CEO in the story who makes that claim.

"These aren't the droids you're looking for."

In writing this, I assume you are selling something you believe in and you honestly feel will benefit your customer. These questions are powerful tools of cognitive impact, but certainly not Jedi Mind Tricks.

Unfortunately, the Counterfactual Hypothetical question has been used shamefully in the past. The most notorious use of the Counterfactual Hypothetical is its use in Push-Polling. Push-Polling is political telemarketing masquerading as an opinion poll. It uses counterfactuals in a hypothetical question to influence voters' perceptions of candidates.

In his 1994 bid for Texas Governor, George W. Bush's campaign used it against Ann

Richards. On the phone, voters were asked, "Would you be more or less likely to vote for Governor Richards if you knew that lesbians dominated on her staff."[52]

A few years later, in the South Carolina Republican Primary voters were asked, "Would you be more likely or less likely to vote for John McCain for president if you knew he had fathered an illegitimate black child?"[53] This was the Bush campaign again. Karl Rove reportedly, "had no interest in the actual percentages in the poll, the goal was to suggest that McCain had a black child,"[54] which was not true. The results of the South Carolina primary ended McCain's momentum in his bid for President.

---

[52] "This Week in the Polls - How Mobile Apps Enhance the Power of Political Polls/surveys." *Enterprise Mobile Backend as a Service | Kinvey*. N.p., 01 Apr. 2017. Web. 14 Apr. 2018.
[53] Davis, Richard H. "The Anatomy of a Smear Campaign." Boston.com. The Boston Globe, 21 Mar. 2004. Web. 17 Dec. 2017.
[54] "The Anatomy of a Smear Campaign - Rove's Push Polls." Daily Kos. N.p., n.d. Web. 17 Dec. 2017.

Mixing a Message

In using the Counterfactual Hypothetical, first ensure the prospect has the material, (the narrative 'facts'), necessary to build the right answer. The most effective way to deliver those 'facts' is through true stories. These stories are usually about previous customers and their experience working with your sales people and your company. You will develop stories around:

- Eliminating the personal risk the prospect fears
- How your product or service enables the prospect to be heroic

- How the product or service does wonderful things for the buying company

Before crafting a story, identify what the story's narrative needs to contain and convey. The rule is to convey one idea, though you can bake secondary concepts into the narrative as long as they don't impede the main idea.

Let's look at two approaches to crafting a story. One is based on the method described in *Made To Stick* by Chip and Dan Heath. Their formula is S.U.C.C.E.S: Simple, Unexpected, Concrete, Credible, Emotional, Story. I am going to add an orthographically correct final 'S' at the end for Short.

Simple.

Using simple language to convey simple concepts makes it easier for the listener's brain to comprehend[55]. It also makes the

---

[55] Oppenheimer, Daniel M. "Consequences of Erudite Vernacular Utilized Irrespective of Necessity: Problems with Using Long Words Needlessly." *Applied Cognitive Psychology* 20.2 (2006): 139-56.

information conveyed seem more truthful[56]. Simple language helps the prospect build affinity with the subject being communicated. And that lets the prospect develop confidence around subsequent judgments. Thus, we follow the rule Keep It Simple Stupid (KISS)[57].

Unexpectedness

Unexpectedness is what gives a story its juice. It is what grabs attention. It is what makes magic-tricks magical, and why people like jokes so much. For some reason, the reveal of a trick or punch-line tickles the pleasure centers of the brain. It works when we set up the surprise at the beginning of the story and reveal it at the end.

---

[56] Reber, Rolf, and Norbert Schwarz. "Effects of Perceptual Fluency on Judgments of Truth." *Consciousness and Cognition* 8.3 (1999): 338-42.

[57] According to Wikipedia "The acronym was reportedly coined by Kelly Johnson, lead engineer at the Lockheed Skunk Works (creators of the Lockheed U-2 and SR-71 Blackbird spy planes, among many others).

Often surprise is described as violating our expectations. That's not exactly what the goal is here. When it comes to cognitive impact, unexpectedness must be wielded slightly differently.

The most influential surprise is one in which the listener has an idea of what the reveal might be, without knowing for sure.[58] It's a fine line. It doesn't work if the listener already knows the reveal, or if the reveal is too obvious. It also doesn't work if the surprise at the end could not have been anticipated. You want your narrative to unfold so the listener develops an expectation of what might be coming. It works best if the listener has a categorical idea of the outcome, not a specific idea.

For example, the listener gets a hint early in the story and expects that one of the four

---

[58] Whittlesea, Bruce W. A., and Lisa D. Williams. "The Discrepancy-attribution Hypothesis: II. Expectation, Uncertainty, Surprise, and Feelings of Familiarity." *Journal of Experimental Psychology: Learning, Memory, and Cognition* 27.1 (2001): 14-33.

people mentioned at the beginning of the story will be the source of the solution. As long as that turns out to be true at the category level (one of the four), the story works. In hindsight, listeners are likely to convince themselves that they knew more than they actually did. They might come to believe that they knew who it was all along. That is an ideal outcome for the cognitive impact story. The surprise is something 'they knew all along,' when in fact they could only guess. It delivers a sense of gratification that makes the story more personal.

Set up the story so it contains enough to trigger this surprising component.

Concrete

Concrete details pull the listener into the story. These are the sensory details that allow the listeners to imagine themselves in the story.

"When the rain finally stopped, they stepped outside and could smell that wonderful fresh smell of a recent rain in a forest."

A single sentence can accomplish scene

setting. Once the listener is pulled into the story, they are in for the duration. (This notion is consistent with our earlier discussion of making some action more visceral in a question.)

Creditability

Credibility is necessary, especially in a sales situation. If the story is supposed to be true, then it better be soundly true. The best advice is to use true stories because they can be defended.

Emotion

Emotion in a story is important, but can be subtle. You want to create it without being too overt. In the previous chapter's example, the audience was the purchasing manager. We expect a purchasing manager to empathize with the purchasing manager in the story. Since the outcome was good for the purchasing manager in the story, the listener will likely share that feeling.

Story

Story is the second 's' in Chip and Dan Heath's model. It's a narrative designed to interest, amuse, and influence the listener. In the Heath brother's model, the narrative should contain the other elements; be simple, create delightful surprise, be concrete, credible, and finally, be short.

Short

This is my added final 'S'. Keep it short. If you practice telling a story in two minutes, telling it in a sales call will likely take three. Remember, **Good things, when short, are twice as good**.

When I work with teams, I take them through an exercise that helps them write a useful story. We use the form below.

The key theme could be the removal of an identified risk for the prospect, how the prospect becomes a hero, or how the solution works for the company and the prospect.

Imagine the story on page 102 had been developed in this way. Remember, we're building a foundation for the Counterfactual Hypothetical we will ask later.

Step	Outline Items
Key Theme: The impact on the prospect	
Point of Conflict or the Problem	
Characters	
Concreteness (Set the scene)	
Key Narrative Facts	
How it turned out	
The Hook (Unexpectedness)	

Key Theme

The impact on the prospect: the prospect sees an opportunity to be the hero because the cooker enables the company to be more innovative.

Point of Conflict or the Problem

The cooker is taking 8 hours to clean, much longer than promised.

Characters

Pat (our salesperson), the Purchasing Manager at the company, CEO of the client company, and in a supporting role, the CFO.

Concreteness (Set the scene)
There's a loud hum of activity and the company is cooking something that smells good.

Key Narrative Facts:
- Pat gets a call from the purchasing manager.
- There's a problem with cooker's cleanup time.
- Pat visits the plant but can't find the problem.
- The CEO stops by and explains there's no problem, they're using the cooker to innovate.

How it turned out: The purchasing manager is a hero to CEO.

The Hook (Unexpectedness):
Something funny happened to Pat a couple of weeks ago.

We could develop a stronger hook, but it's

not necessary given the context. Since the conversation that led up to telling the story was about the short cleanup time for the SlurryThermal cooker, the prospect will anticipate that there was no problem with the cleanup time. The surprise is the purchasing manager became a hero. That will provide a little emotional lift to prospects and help them later use the information in crafting their answer to the Counterfactual Hypothetical question.

To infinity and beyond!

The other approach I use with people is the PIXAR approach. I encourage anyone who wants to practice creating stories to go to the Kahn Academy website and watch the Pixar "story structure" video.[59]

The Pixar based approach, which I modified slightly, has you develop the hook as the last element even though you will

---

[59] The Khan Academy has a program put together with Pixar on crafting stories. The third part is about story structure.
https://www.khanacademy.org/partnercontent/pixar/storytelling/story-structure/v/piab-storystructure?

place it at the beginning of the story.

Step	Outline Items
Key Theme: The impact on the prospect	
Once Upon a Time	
Every Day	
Until one day	
Because of that	
Because of that	
Until finally	
The Hook (Unexpectedness)	

When applying this approach to the story, you might end up with a somewhat different story. Two different approaches create the opportunity to tell the story in different ways. You can choose the way that feels most comfortable. Most story tellers favor one method over the other, but I encourage you to try the other method whenever the story doesn't feel perfect. It just takes a minute to fill out the outline and might enrich how you tell the story.

Here is the sample story outline using the PIXAR method.

Key Theme

The impact on the prospect: The prospect sees an opportunity to be the hero because the cooker enables the company to be more innovative.

Once Upon a Time

Six months earlier, a purchasing manager at a food company bought a SlurryThermal cooker. The purchasing manager went out on a limb in recommending this new technology.

Every Day

Things appeared to be going well with the new cooker.

Until one day

The CFO shows up in the purchasing managers office to show him a production report that says the new cooker is taking eight hours to clean instead of the 10 minutes promised by the manufacturer. The purchasing manager makes an angry call to the salesperson, Pat, complaining about the cleanup time problem.

Because of that
Pat pays a visit to the factory floor and checks the cooker, but cannot figure out why it's not cleaning up in the specified 10 minutes. Then the CEO of the company comes walking by and asks what is going on.

Because of that
The CEO clears up the error and praises the purchasing manager for buying a product that lets the company innovate far more productively than before.

Until finally
The purchasing manager feels great that he bought the SlurryThermal cooker!

The Hook (unexpectedness)
Something funny that happened a couple of weeks ago to salesperson Pat.

In *Outsell*, I wrote out the whole story in order for you to see it. It's not what I would normally do. I have about 50 stories I use for sales. None are written down. I store the outlines of the stories in my brain. So, when I tell a story, it is out of my working brain, not memorized. When stories are memorized, they sound memorized. Thus, I encourage you not to memorize a story even if you feel compelled to write it out completely. Having a story's outline saved on your computer in a 'story outlines' folder will later remind you of a good story that you might have forgotten or put aside. There's no such thing as having too many stories. You'll only use two to three in a normal sales pitch, but it helps to have a pool of selections.

Lastly, practice telling a story until you feel comfortable that it flows and you're not going to forget some key ingredient. Keep in mind the story you tell is to enable the telling of the more influential story. That's the story your prospect tells in answering the Counterfactual Hypothetical question.

A Sales Force Marches On Its Questions.

You now have a basic understanding of how to use three types of questions, how to craft them, and when to use them:

- Peak/End Questions
- Intent Questions
- Counterfactual Hypothetical Questions

There are a handful of additional things to improve sales strategy.

When working directly with companies, I include more things they can do with their marketing, pricing, collateral, competitors and positioning that will improve outcomes for the sales force. The expression, 'an army marches on its stomach,' is about all the support services that equip the front line soldier to do his or her job well. Likewise, there are many things such as operations, design, marketing, and customer service, that enhance or undermine the business' front-line: its sales force.

While there is a lot more to it, here is just a handful of things you can do that support asking the three question types in a sale.

A good question is worth a thousand statements.

Examine your existing sales collateral and look for opportunities to replace statements with questions. Construct those questions such that they start with the proposition contained in the statement you are replacing. Recall that propositions are the parts of statements that can be true or false. Include true ones. Propositions contained inside questions are more believable, and are less likely to be challenged in the mind of the listener.

For example, I could replace the statement:
"Sales P.A.R. Excellence will increase your sales effectiveness."
With:
"If your sales team were to use a set of tools like Sales P.A.R. Excellence, which have proven to increase sales, how would your company be able to ramp up production to meet more demand?"

Word to the wise

When developing marketing materials or making questions more salient, words matter. The content of a question can influence how someone evaluates an action or event. This was demonstrated in a study done by Elizabeth Loftus and John Palmer. They showed videos of car accidents to students and asked them a series of questions about what they observed. For example, "Give an account of the accident you have just seen." Among the questions, the one being tested was: "About how fast were the cars going when they hit each other?" For different random groups of students, the word 'hit' was replaced with one of the words: *smashed, collided, bumped,* or *contacted.* The choice of verb influenced the students' recollection of speed.[60]

Verb Used	Average Speed Estimate
Smashed	40.8
Collided	39.3
Bumped	38.1
Hit	34.0
Contacted	31.8

In legal depositions, questions framed like this and asked of eyewitnesses can lead to

---

[60] Loftus, Elizabeth F., and John C. Palmer. "Reconstruction of Automobile Destruction: An Example of the Interaction between Language and Memory." Journal of Verbal Learning and Verbal Behavior 13.5 (1974): 585-89. Print.

the erroneous recall of events that can change the judgment of guilt or innocence[61]. In a sales situation, your choice of words can impact the emotional content in the listener's thinking.

Ask a better question, and the customer will beat a path to your doorstep.

Look at the existing questions. We want to get the prospect talking. In fact, if you're doing all the talking, you're on the wrong side of the table. Questions that start with a verb ('is', 'are', 'do', 'can', or with the words 'could', 'should', or 'would') often can be answered with one word. Try to avoid asking such questions, as you want the prospect to say more. Kick their emotional engine into gear by getting them to talk. Ask questions that call for an open-ended response. Typically those are questions that start with 'how', 'what', 'where', 'when', and

---

[61] Fitzsimons, Gavan J., and Baba Shiv. "Non-conscious and Contaminative Effects of Hypothetical Questions on Subsequent Decision Making." Journal of Consumer Research 28.2 (2001): 224-38.

'who'. 'How' is probably the most likely question to get an open-ended response. You can also get open-ended responses when beginning a sentence with words or phases such as 'describe', 'explain', 'tell me about', or 'what do you think about?'

You can get single word response to 'what', 'where', 'when', and 'who' questions. For example, "Who did this?" A good rule of thumb is to practice forming questions that don't allow for one word, or single phrase responses.

Brainstorm ways to make your existing questions more influential. Let the question paint a picture for your prospect. For example:

You're going to select a solution like Sales P.A.R. Excellence strategy that been shown to deliver a strong lift in sales. Let's say that's what you selected as your best solution, when could we expect to hear from you, and how would you let us know that?

In the example question above, I included

the <u>benefit</u> of using Sales P.A.R. Excellence tools – '*a lift in sales*'. This gives the question a little emotional kick, and those kicks build up like a wave gathering power as it crosses the ocean.

Additionally, the question contains something salient for the prospect – it's the image of them communicating with us their selection of our solution. It's obviously an intent question that makes it slightly more likely that this will be the outcome.

Take time working through questions to convert them from solely information gathering tools to ones that are also influential.

Be careful what you ask for, as you'll likely get it.

Throw out any question you cannot defend as being either influential or crucial to gathering information. Don't throw out questions you use to build a relationship with customers. You might find a better way to ask them. Asking questions to draw out something personal, starts to create a bond between salesperson and prospect.

Occasionally, that results in the entire sales call to be absorbed by a prospect's personal story. You get what you ask for. Sometimes that's not so bad where the relationship is important. With a good relationship, a salesperson will get more chances to step up to the plate, and more likely to get a hit.

Lastly, the "IKEA effect"

The prospect is going to make a decision. To the extent prospects build that decision by constructing its elements, they will 'own' it.

How much do we love what we build? For many, the feeling of accomplishment serves as an important personal motivator. To answer that question, Michael Norton of Harvard, Daniel Mochon of Tulane, and Dan Ariely of Duke got together and conducted a set of experiments[62].

---

[62] Norton, Michael I., Daniel Mochon, and Dan Ariely. "The 'IKEA Effect': When Labor Leads to Love." *SSRN Electronic Journal* (2011):

OUTSELL

In the first experiment, members in one group of participants were asked to assemble plain black IKEA storage boxes. The other group was given pre-assembled boxes and asked to inspect them. Then, individuals from both groups were asked to come up with a bid number for what they would be willing to pay for the box. A random price would then be drawn out. If the participant's bid was equal to, or greater than that random price, then the participant could buy the box. Otherwise they were not allowed to buy the box.

As you might expect, the builder group submitted bids that averaged 63 percent higher that the non-builder group. After all, they had built them and had more 'ownership' of the boxes.

Since the IKEA box was kind of a utilitarian product, the experimenters wanted to find out how people valued something where they put in more creative effort. This time they had subjects make either an origami frog or crane from provided paper and instructions. When they were done, the builders were told they could bid on their creation using the same bidding structure as used for the IKEA boxes. (You can imagine what some of these frogs and cranes ended up looking like.) Next, a second group of people was brought in and given the chance to bid on these frogs and cranes to purchase them. It turned out that the builders valued their creations nearly five times more than the non-builders.

We take pride in our own creations, and tend to overvalue their worth in the world.

It turns out people emotionally 'own' things they build. The question types in the Sales P.A.R. Excellence strategy are designed to allow your prospects to build up to their decision. Your Counterfactual Hypothetical questions are a big part of that process. They are designed in part to allow the prospect to put the pieces together. When the prospect finally makes the decision, they will own it, for better or worse.

OUTSELL

Good Luck and Good Selling. Remember,

Questions are a salesperson's best friend.

And,

An ounce of asking is worth a pound of telling.

ABOUT THE AUTHOR

Bill Burnett is an experienced executive with a wealth of international experience having lived in six countries outside the USA and worked with local teams in all sorts of cultural settings in more than 60 additional countries. At Diners Club International, leveraging his background in running the 'factory' of the back-office, Bill spent 10 years as Head of Global Operation, and another 5 as Senior Vice President Strategic Initiatives. As a perpetual student of leadership and human psychology he's brought out the best in individuals, irrespective of reporting relationship. In Diners Club, he had the primary responsibility for innovation in a company that claimed the most innovations in the industry. Bill understands that the top ideas come from both collaborative teams and curious individuals and often from the most unlikely brains.

He is married to Linda Britton. They have three children, George 32, Madeleine 30, and Charlie, 22. Bill has written four other business books, and numerous articles. He holds a BA from the University of Northern Colorado, and a Masters in International Business from the Moore School at the University of South Carolina. www.linkedin.com/in/billburnett/

OUTSELL

www.ingramcontent.com/pod-product-compliance
Lightning Source LLC
Chambersburg PA
CBHW020425220526
45464CB00002B/566